Contents

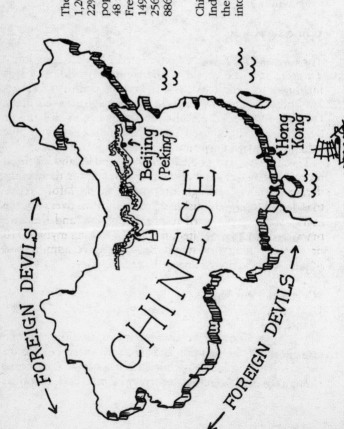

The Chinese population is 1,200 million, which is nearly 22% of the world's total population (compared with 48 million English; 57 million French, 80 million Germans, 149 million Russians, 256 million Americans and 886 million Indians).

China is 3 times the size of India and slightly larger than the United States, but could fit into Russia 1¾ times.

FOREIGN DEVILS →

CHINESE

Beijing (Peking)

Hong Kong

← FOREIGN DEVILS

← FOREIGN DEVILS →

Nationalism and Identity

The Chinese are a colourful lot. They used to be called the Yellow Peril. In the 1950s it was fashionable to call them the Blue Ants. At various times they are referred to as the Red Menace. They are not as black as they are sometimes painted, nor as grey and drab as some would have you believe.

Foreign Devils

The Chinese call China *Zhongguo* (the Middle Kingdom). To them it is the centre of the civilized world, and it is inhabited by people. All else is 'outside country', barbarian and inhabited by oceanic (i.e. foreign) devils. Black Devils live in Africa, Red-haired Devils live in Holland or Scandinavia, High-nosed Devils have white skin and blue eyes and live in Europe and America and Australia.

These devils are not expected to understand civilized human behaviour, and allowance is made for their blundering manners, though they have to be loftily reprimanded if their childishness makes them overstep the mark. Some devils learn to speak Chinese, and they are marvelled at and exhibited, much as a talking mynah bird or a performing flea might be – they are admitted to human society, but can never be real people.

Forewarned

The Chinese know, have always known, that they are the custodians of the greatest and most advanced culture on earth. Time and again barbarian hordes have conquered China only to be themselves overwhelmed and absorbed by the strength and weight of the culture they sought to control. On the periphery of the Middle Kingdom the Koreans and the Vietnamese and the Japanese all learned to defer to Chinese culture, and they adopted its writing system, its philosophies, and some of its customs, confirming the Chinese in their belief in their own superiority.

The Chinese do not suffer from xenophobia. They care about other peoples so little that they could not whip up enough energy to be phobic about them. If the leadership says "Go and stone a few foreigners" they will do it, but they can be quite dispassionate about it, which is a consoling thought.

The Chinese do not identify with any other people on earth because they do not believe that there is any people equal to them. For strategic reasons they have lined up with the Third World, just as for strategic reasons they 'adopted' black Africa for a while, but there is no conviction behind their friendship. If they have a particular dislike it is for the Japanese, their invaders during the Pacific War, but they have been able to suppress that dislike, again for strategic and trade reasons.

At heart they do not care about others. They do not even make jokes about them. The butt of Chinese jokes is usually another Chinese, who will be called Ah-Fu (Gormless), or else will be handicapped in some way, or maybe come from another part of China where they speak a strange dialect or have weird customs.

Of all the barbarians who came to China, only the Westerners were strong enough on their own cultural base to resist absorption and surrender, and the result of this match seems to have been a 'score-draw', each side taking from the other and giving as well. So the West took to drinking tea, dressing in silk, eating rhubarb from porcelain dishes, creating civil service examinations, and

enjoying flowers and shrubs which the Chinese had culti-
vated for centuries. The Chinese built railways, learned to
play poker and to smoke cigarettes, adopted the scientific
method, adapted socialism to their own tastes, and found
that international trade could be profitable for them after
all.

But it only seems to have been a draw. The Chinese
have a long perspective on history and they are unshaken
in their conviction that extra-time will see them come out
the victors.

Character

There are an awful lot of Chinese people and they live in
an awfully big place (about the same size as all of
Western and Eastern Europe combined).

They are as diverse as the Europeans too, so there are
tall, big-boned, Northern Chinese and squat, delicate
Southerners, there are those who are intermixed with
Turkic peoples, with nomadic sheep herders, with southern hill tribesmen, and with lowland Tai agriculturalists.
They live in caves carved from the yellow loess soil, in
brick and granite-slab terrace houses, in mud-brick straw-
thatched huts, in concrete tenement blocks, in tents made
from skins, and in wooden buildings with lattice-work
windows 'glazed' with translucent paper. They speak
many different languages, dress in different costumes, eat
a huge variety of foods.

Despite this variety there is a strong Chinese-ness about
them, and it is made up of arrogance, nepotism, con-
formism and fatalism.

Arrogance

All Chinese people know that they are the cream of mankind (not God's own people, because no god is big enough to own them, it is they who have created the gods), and they would have a hearty pity for all other people if it should ever enter their heads to consider them (but it doesn't). An unconcerned arrogance is the firm foundation of the Chinese character. A non-Chinese cannot insult a Chinese any more than a two year-old child can insult you: if the insultee does not recognise the capacity and standing of the insulter, how can there be an insult?

Nepotism

All Chinese operate on a system of tight insider networks (family and friends), mercilessly exploiting them and in turn being exploited by them, but relying on them to stay afloat in the vast troubled sea of Chinese society where no-one else will lend a hand to help you into the lifeboat.

Chinese friendships are almost indestructible; they last through thick and thin, as do kinship relationships. They have to last, for the isolated individual drowns. Intense loyalty to a small group is therefore part of the Chinese character.

Conformism

All Chinese are inured to hierarchy, they suppress initiative and rely on direction from above, in turn suppressing independence in those beneath them. This is how the Chinese leadership can do so much damage, why corrupt emperors have brought down their dynasties, why profligate heads of families have ruined their descendants without protest from their grown children.

Fatalism

All Chinese have fatalism heavily built in. If things are going well for you, accept, enjoy to the full, and ride the wave of luck for all you are worth; if they are going badly, it is not your fault, accept, suffer, and hope that the ill wave will soon run out of force. There is little justice seen in the meting out of rewards and punishments in the Chinese world. Chinese gods are not expected to help those who most merit it, they throw their weight behind those who bribe them with the most expensive sacrifices – just like Chinese officials.

Phlegmatism

The Chinese live packed together in densities which would send Westerners to shrinks in droves. They tolerate the presence and idiosyncrasies of their families and their neighbours with a patience and ease which other races could not hope to emulate.

It helps that they have always been phlegmatic – it is not something new forced upon them by their swollen population. In a country where agriculture counted for so much, it was considered wasteful to build on the land, and village housing was cramped together on small plots. Even in the great walled cities which housed the administrators of the empire, spacious housing was the exception rather than the rule.

They have achieved their high level of toleration by learning to cultivate a serene unawareness of other people's existence. On the positive side, they genuinely do not notice that potentially irritating finger-tapping which X does all day long. On the negative, they will push past to get ahead of you on the pavement and then slow to a crawl so that you fall over them – you have ceased to exist as soon as you are out of their view and it is up to you to look out for yourself.

They smile under all circumstances, happy, tragic or in between. They accept and yield and tone down emotion and avoid direct confrontation. How else could so many temperaments live with each other in so confined a space?

Of course, they are not really unaware of the existence of others – unconsciously they are highly sensitive to the almost invisible signals which others put out and which indicate the boundaries of acceptable intrusion into their personal space. Because of this a Chinese is able in an uncanny way to anticipate what you are about to ask or do – he reads your intention before you have consciously formed it.

Unconscious sensitivity and studied unawareness normally do the trick. However, society occasionally has to pay a price for the generally prevailing equanimity – if patience and toleration are pushed too far, something snaps and the inscrutable Chinese becomes a raging, uncontrolled and uncontrollable animal, he picks up a kitchen chopper and swings at everyone in sight. In two minutes half his family and several chance passers-by are lying dead in a sea of blood.

Truthfulness

If lying is 'economy with the truth', the Chinese economy has always been in a dire state of inflation. Confucius told lies: when he did not want to see someone he invented a reason why he was busy.

Lying saves the embarrassment which might be caused by refusal. "Could you lend me a few dollars?" "Oh, I'm so sorry, my grandfather has just died and I myself have had to borrow to put a deposit on a coffin." No-one is fooled, but it would be grossly rude to challenge the accuracy of the excuse.

The unwary foreigner, taught from birth that truth and bluntness are important, is at a terrible disadvantage in dealing with the practised evasions of master manipulators who put ends before means.

Modesty

No Chinese will ever confess to doing anything well or to possessing anything valuable or to being anything other than despicable and unworthy of praise. On the other hand, no Chinese will fail to praise with fulsome attention to detail the deeds, attributes and possessions of almost everyone else he or she meets.

"How beautiful and talented your thousand pieces of gold (daughter) is" he gushes. "Oh, my goods on which I will lose my investment (daughter)" replies his friend, "she is ugly and good for nothing at all."

"What a splendid meal that was. Thank you very much indeed," says the guest. "It was just scraps from the kitchen, not fit for your noble lips to touch. I deserve to die for producing it," wails the host.

The innocent foreigner walks into this game unaware of the rules. "How wonderfully you speak Chinese. Just like a native," exclaims the polite recipient of a garbled diatribe, meanwhile trying to work out what it might possibly have been supposed to mean and what country the speaker sounded like a native of. "Oh, yes, I speak it as well as this because I have an ear for languages, and I always came top of my class in Chinese," proudly responds the native of Puffup, Missouri. He retires from the encounter happy and confirmed in his self-esteem, but the Chinese, bemused at the appalling conceit of this breaker of social rules, is beside himself with glee at the obscenities and howlers which Mr Puffup has mistakenly uttered while thinking he was discussing the weather.

Even worse off is the poor foreigner who does understand the rules, because he can be made to suffer. "How elegantly you write your Chinese characters ..." the hypocritical celestial warbles, and the miserable foreign devil is forced to contemplate the sorry wobbly messes into which his high nose has just been metaphorically rubbed. "Oh, no, they're awful" he has in politeness and in honesty to reply, and he knows that he has been scored off. But it doesn't stop there, the persecution goes on: "Compared with my weak and rustic calligraphy, yours has such power and sophistication." With sinking heart the Westerner launches into a panegyric on the sublime beauty of his tormentor's hand and how beside it his own writing looks like the muddy trails left by an arthritic panda drunk on bamboo sap. And all the time he had known it was coming, had known that he would end up having to give the praise and cede the superiority which his Chinese sparring partner had so humbly coveted from the moment he had initiated the exchange.

"Of course, we Chinese are very modest", boasted one individual, which summed it all up quite well.

Addiction to Noise

The Chinese do not understand silence. It is as distasteful to them as are loud decibels to most Westerners. Silence means loneliness – if there was anyone around there would be noise, it is as simple as that. The Chinese word for 'having a good time' is *re-nao*, which means literally 'it's hot and noisy'. If it is quiet then by definition a good time is not being had.

One rarely sees a lone Chinese, they always do things in company. If someone is ill in bed the last thing he or she wants is to be left there to suffer and recuperate in peace. Friends and relations come pouring in to shout and brawl over the bedspace, discussing the symptoms, giving advice on how to get better, and consoling the dying with hopeless shakes of the head, unable to speak because of the noise of the coffin being nailed together in the next room to the accompaniment of the jolly whistling and coarse banter of the undertaker's men as they rejoice at being in work again.

Restaurants in the West have deeper carpets and more sound-baffles the more expensive they are. Chinese restaurants at all price levels have tiled floors and walls for better sound enhancement: the waiters shout out orders, the diners talk at the tops of their voices, the children run around screaming at each other between the tables. "It's very noisy in here" shouts the overwhelmed Western guest to his Chinese host. "Yes, good restaurant, isn't it?" he replies.

The favourite game of the Chinese is mahjong. It can be played with playing cards, but no-one bothers to do so, it's too quiet that way. Instead they have specially-made tables with resonant tops to make the slamming down of the tiles as loud and exciting as possible. Ask any visitor to China what sound is most nostalgic and he will answer for certain, "the sound of mahjong being played, and the racket as the tiles are washed (shuffled) between games". People play all night, sometimes sitting up for 48-hour sessions. Do the neighbours complain? Not a bit of it – they don't even hear it, except maybe as a pleasant lullaby to help their sleep.

People are surrounded by noise all day and all night, they make it themselves, they are at once hooked on it and impervious to it. If the fortune-teller or the Almanac says that 3 a.m. is a good time for holding a little ceremony to celebrate the completion of the building of your house, then that is when you must hold the ceremony, and since no such ritual would be worth having without firecrackers and noise then you will let off firecrackers and make plenty of noise. Do the neighbours phone the police? Of course not. They turn over in their beds with a warm and happy smile on their untroubled faces.

Fortunately the Chinese, like all Mongoloid peoples, do not produce ear-wax. They have instead a white powdery substance. It can only be surmised that this developed as an antidote to noise, somehow acting as a filter so that the surrounding din does not damage the ear-drums.

Only a culture with extraordinary noise-toleration could have dreamed up and persisted with Chinese music. The cacophony of cymbals, drums, gongs, hollow blocks, fiddles strung with the guts of hyenas which have died of laryngitis, and wind instruments modelled on party balloons with rude stoppers has to be heard to be believed. For many visitors to China it has been the last thing they heard before deafness set in.

Attitudes and Values

Chinese people brought up and working in the fervent years of revolution and post-revolutionary political movements knew a sense of purpose and unity and unremitting unselfish labour directed to the building of a strong and advanced new state. Much of that enthusiasm was misdirected and wasted by incompetent leadership which while claiming that it was of the people put itself above the people and out of touch with reality.

Today there is a new enthusiasm, not for politics or state-building, but for money. Now it is considered cool to be rich, and along with that come corruption, nepotism, fraud, greed, robbery, and a lust for the good things of life. McDonalds, motor-bikes, smart clothes, Rolex watches, night clubs, sauna and massage parlours, expensive restaurants, karaoke bars, large and expensively furnished houses – conspicuous consumption is the order of the day, especially for the young and quick.

The middle-aged and elderly sit back aghast and wonder why they fought a bloody revolution and sweated so hard in order that the young can revert to the lifestyle of pre-Revolutionary Shanghai. The young are too busy making and spending money to wonder whether it is wise; like the grasshopper of fable, they are fiddling through the summer without a thought to how the country they are playing in is to be run in the hard winter which will surely follow.

There is little conception of social conscience – how can Ah-Wong relate to the troubles and needs of someone 3000 miles away who happens also to be Chinese? For that matter how can he spare concern for someone three streets away? He has plenty of his own problems to worry about. If you want his attention, you must pay for it.

"You would like to sell your goods to my company? Certainly, sir, but why should I buy from you and not from Ah-Lee? Did you say a complimentary holiday for two to the Bahamas? Well, as a matter of fact, I believe we do need those components you make, and the doctor said I ought to take a holiday. My secretary can come with me – she'll be able to ...ah... help me with the correspondence."

Religion

China used to be described in the 19th century as 'the land of 400,000,000 Buddhists'. Of course that description would not fit now – there were thirty years of suppression of religious practice from 1949 on, and the population is now three times as big.

But even in the 19th century it was a misleading statement. There probably were 400 million Buddhists, but there were also 400 million ancestor worshippers, 400 million Taoists, and 400 million nature worshippers too.

The Chinese have always been wide-ranging in their beliefs, seeing no reason for exclusivity, and being perfectly happy to worship any god who comes along provided he (or she) produces satisfactory results. Worship is a two-way process, a contract which both sides must stick to. If a hard-up peasant is to lay out good money for food, candles and incense, he expects the recipient of these goods to reciprocate with blessings in the way of prosperity, success, good health and good luck at gambling. If none of these results is obtained, he will worship another god instead.

Religious practice is apparently more important than religious belief. If serious thought were given to belief there might be some doubt for a Chinese, as an ancestor worshipper, about the efficacy of worshipping his dead parents, grandparents, great-grandparents and so on when, as a Buddhist, he assumes these same ancestors to have been reborn as someone or something else.

But, he says, don't worry about thinking too much – go ahead and worship them and the various gods of Buddhism as well. Who can be sure that they aren't all in possession of some spiritual powers which will benefit you? Anyway, it's not our fault if the gods are in conflict: that's their business and they can sort it out amongst themselves.

The Family

In the past, Chinese families could be a monstrous size. It was considered proper for sons when they married to stay at home and raise their own families within the family, and their sons in turn would do the same. The daughters born to the family would of course be married out to be wives in other families. After several generations of only moderate reproductivity there could be a very large number of people all living together.

Controlling such a group was not easy. The law said that the authority and powers of the family head (father, grandfather or whoever he might be) were almost absolute, and beneath him every man, woman and child was taught his or her place in the pecking order, so that if the authority chain were observed there could never be any fighting or argument – only equals could argue, and the hierarchy produced no equals.

Bottom of the heap were the women, but if they lived long enough and were lucky enough they could end up by having authority over their sons' wives. Then watch out all daughters-in-law – after years of abuse and repression, mother-in-law had got her head. Guess who she took it out on.

The family shackled the individual with chains which he/she could not afford to break, because the enchained group was also a reliable source of strength and support. The family shared its fortune and its fate. At times it was the law that if one member committed a crime the whole family or any other member of it could be punished. The filial son could go to the execution ground in place of his father the criminal; treason by one meant death for all. On the other side of the coin, if one member became rich everyone shared in it.

The term 'the family' meant only the male-based family.

17

Your mother's family meant almost nothing to you, but your father's family was your whole life. A man could not marry anyone who had the same surname as his father because they could be related to him and that would be incest, but he could marry his mother's brother's daughter (his first cousin) with no fear of disapproval or punishment because she was of a quite different surname and therefore not related at all.

In fact, high infant mortality rates, disease, war, poverty and social disorder combined to check the size of the family, and where a family did manage to multiply, the mother-in-law problem was sometimes too much for the young, who would move out rather than put up with it.

The One Child Family

In the 1950s China had a birth control policy of sorts. Admittedly it was rather stop-go and sometimes a bit loony; for instance, one senior herbalist adviser actually recommended to the government that doses of live tadpoles swallowed regularly by a woman on a daily basis would prevent conception and if persisted with would produce sterility for at least five years. However, Mao Tse-tung contrived a new Thought (something he did frequently) and decided that China's strength lay in her people, so the more of them there were, the stronger she would be. With such encouragement and without television to distract them, the people got down with commendable fervour to the serious business of reproduction. In 1949 the population was about 450 million, and by 1995 it was estimated to have passed the 1,200 million mark and still be climbing.

Even the most dedicated believer in the infallibility of Mao could see that the Great Helmsman had given them a bum steer, and attempts were made to change course. Barefoot doctors toured the countless villages to instruct the wondering populace on what it was that was causing the epidemic of babies. Birth control devices were offered free, abortions were encouraged, and nosy street committee women (the street committee was a kind of Neighbourhood Watch whose remit did not stop at other peoples' front doors) stopped guarding bicycles and watched their neighbours' cycles instead. Huge posters went up advertising the splendours of the small and hence wealthy family. By the late 1970s the One Child Policy had appeared, late marriage was encouraged, financial inducements were being offered to couples to be sterilised after the birth of their first child, and public opinion was harnessed to bring pressure on anyone who was selfish enough to want more than one. Some zealous officials seized the chance to perform forced abortions on those women who tried to contravene the Policy.

Even if all couples had only had one child the population would have gone on rising for many years just because so many of them were at the child-bearing age, but in the countryside where controls were less strict it was seldom possible to persuade people that multiple births were not a good thing and the safest form of insurance against starvation in old age.

In the cities (which account for only about 30% of the population) the policy has been comparatively successful, and much propaganda is made of the red-cheeked rotund little figures dressed up to the nines being shown off in the park by their adoring parents. All hopes are invested in these 'little emperors', and don't they know it. They swagger and demand, are overfed, overclothed and overprotected, throw tantrums (and anything else that comes to hand), and produce apoplexy in those many old-fashioned adults who, indifferent to political correctness,

19

itch to take a bamboo rod to their spoiled backsides.

If the policy continues, the Chinese will have invented a new kind of society in which there are no brothers and sisters, no aunts, no uncles, no cousins, no nephews and no nieces, a society where the only relatives a child has will be parents and two sets of grandparents vying to outdo each other in indulgence. Such a child will probably not grow up feeling responsible for these six people in their old age, and in any case it would hardly be economically possible for one to support six on a nationwide basis. Too many people. Too few children.

Unfortunately the good Chairman had to keep his celestial appointment with Marx before he could produce another Thought to solve the problem.

The Home

The Chinese do not pay much attention to the physical home in which they live, probably because few can afford to do so. Housing is nearly always inadequate, belongings are crammed in wherever they can be found room, and the people fit in to the remaining gaps. Entertaining is done in restaurants, not at home.

There is hardly any point in being houseproud under the circumstances. In Hong Kong, which instituted a massive cheap public housing programme in the 1950s, it was found that very few of the tenants who made good had any intention of moving out to better quality housing; they became socially mobile but not residentially mobile. Be-suited businessmen with large cars continued to live in very basic flats which had been intended as temporary emergency homes for the least advantaged.

Of course, there always has been the lucky minority who could afford better quality housing. The maxim says that 'Wooden doors should match with wooden doors, and bamboo gates with bamboo gates', meaning that people should marry within the same social level, or to put it more plainly within the same wealth level. This is very sage advice which has little to do with snobbery and much to do with basic human nature – otherwise the poorer family would be round all the time trying to borrow money from the richer.

Divorce

Divorce used to be a male prerogative – he could divorce her but she could not divorce him. Grounds for divorce were not terribly difficult to find and came under seven heads: failure to bear a son (her fault, of course), lascivious conduct (including laziness), failure to serve parents-in-law, theft, jealousy, talking too much, and incurable disease. In practice, divorce was very rare, not because wives did not talk too much or did not fail to have a son, but because the problems caused between the families of the couple would make it not worth the candle.

The Communist Marriage Law was one of the first major pieces of legislation passed by the People's Republic, coming into force in 1950, only one year after the successful revolution. It made divorce available to both men and women, and enabled women to obtain instant divorce if they had an unhappy arranged marriage or if they were in the position of secondary wife (concubine).

Once the initial flush of divorces was over the figures sank to very low levels again. Part of the reason was that the divorce process was not all that easy, and it was necessary to go through compulsory mediation sessions; the mediators often forced couples to stay together, presumably because mediation needed to show a certain success rate too. A British television crew filming in China in the early 1980s was present at a mediation session where a woman was forced to remain with her husband, despite the fact that he was crazy enough to drag her and her new born daughter back to hospital to insist on the doctors sewing the child back into her womb so that he could have a son instead.

By the 1990s the divorce rate had shown a steady rise, marking China's emergence into the international community of dissatisfied spouses.

Education

If there is one value which has remained unchanged over millennia in China it is the respect for scholarship and education. Any Chinese will tell you how tightly bound together are the notions of literacy and culture, and how much they are part of the great Chinese tradition.

Of course there have been times when someone forgot this. The First Emperor of China (who ruled 221-210 BC) in a moment of absent-mindedness buried the pick of the empire's scholars alive, and compounded his mistake by forgetting to dig them up again. Chairman Mao was so keen to hear the views of the scholars that he encouraged them to speak and debate under the banner 'Let a hundred flowers bloom, let a hundred schools of thought contend'; and after they had spoken he also had a memory lapse and sent them away to thought reform school, though how he thought that would cure his bad memory it is hard to see.

The Chinese value scholarship so highly that they find it impossible to believe that anyone who is a scholar could want something as mundane as a living wage. You can tell the teachers and academics of China by their threadbare clothes, consumptive appearance, and habit of walking to school to save the bus fare. The Cantonese, who have a saying for almost everything, say: "*M koong m gaao hok*" –"If you're not poor you don't teach".

Many Chinese subscribe to a remarkable belief that no teacher ever parts with all the knowledge he has. "How could a kung-fu master teach his students to be as good as he is?" they say. "It would be too risky, they might turn on him and defeat him." To the Chinese, knowledge is a disappearing good and the world today is more ignorant than the world of yesterday.

Merry Peasants

The Chinese have managed to perpetuate for 4000 years the myth that farmers are the highest and most important class of society – apart from the leadership, naturally. Confucius said so, his disciples said so, and philosophers, politicians and schoolteachers have gone on saying so.

How romantic the idea of the barefooted peasant skipping muddily but happily at the plough behind his jolly friend, the splay-footed water-buffalo. He rejoices as he considers his esteemed position in the social hierarchy. How joyfully his wife stoops to plant and weed in the paddy-field, the blue, blue sky reflected in its shining mud-rich waters.

Ignore the notorious bad temper of those surly buffalo; forget the mosquitoes which breed in the water and the snails which live in the mud and which plant the debilitating seeds of schistosomiasis in the feet of the toiling masses; pay no attention to the malicious reports which talk of starvation, rack-renting, multiple tax collection, and bureaucratic exploitation: the peasants were and are privileged to do the job.

So convinced were Communist leaders that they sent millions of city people down to the countryside during the Great Proletarian Cultural Revolution of the 1960s and 1970s, an experience which impressed the urbanites deeply enough that they lost no time in sneaking back to their cities, doubtless because they felt themselves unworthy to mix in the exalted company of the farmers.

Being Wealthy

One reason why Hong Kong has been so wildly successful in economic terms has been the fact that every Chinese there, male/female/young/old, knows that wealth can come to anyone. The place is full of self-made millionaires, it has more Rolls Royces per capita than any other country on earth, and a higher proportion of Mercedes to other cars than any other country. It has taller and better and more sophisticated buildings, the best hotels in the world, the greatest density of restaurants, the highest turnover on the horse-race tracks. Wherever you look its wealth shouts at you, and the fat cats purr through the streets in their limousines looking sleekly self-satisfied as they chew their cigars out of the right hand side of their mouths (they cannot use the left side – it is obligatory to be talking on the mobile phone).

And every man, woman and child looks at them not with envy but with admiration; they do not talk of the filthy rich, they merely wonder in hushed tones when (not if) they will be in the same position, and they hurry off home to scheme how to get there.

A Chinese miser is a contradiction in terms, because the whole point of being rich is to be able to show off that you are rich and that means you must spend. In the old days you switched to a permanent opium binge as soon as you had accumulated enough money to do so without ever having to come off the habit again. That way everyone knew that you were rich and you could be respected.

Nowadays you build a new university or make vast donations to worthwhile causes, you join exclusive clubs and buy much-too-big cars and eat exquisite foods (the rarer the better, never mind if it tastes awful). In Canton in the past few years they have taken to garnishing dishes with real gold leaf, because otherwise there is no way in which eating even the most pricey food is sufficiently costly to constitute conspicuous consumption. What all that accumulated gold does to the body in the way of physical harm is hard to tell, but it produces a visible outward glow of pride in the consumer.

From the foundation of the Communist State in 1949 onwards it was dangerous to be even as rich (that is, as poor) as a rich peasant, and there was virtually nothing which could be bought with money if anyone had any. The class system that the classless communists imposed was hereditary, and the children of rich peasants and landlords carried the same stigma as did their parents. But by the 1990s it was alright to be rich again and there were those who were making a great deal of money. Alas, many of them were making it by misusing central and local government funds, while the bewildered, exploited populace milled around, wondering which role model they now had to copy.

One of the texts which Beijing (Peking) language teachers have drilled into their foreign students ever since the Revolution is a parable of a rich man in a splendid carriage drawn by two powerful steeds and driven by a superb coachman. The rich man stops the carriage to ask the way of a poor (but wise) bystander and is told that he is going in the wrong direction. "Never mind", he says, "my horses can go like the wind and will get me any-where in no time at all." "But you are going the wrong way." "What does it matter, I have the best driver in the land." "But the further you go the further from your objective you will be." "So what, I have a great chest of money here with me." And so saying he orders his driver to move on and in no time is lost to sight. "What good are skill, strength and money if you are taking the wrong path" moralises the text book in clear reference to such misguided nations as the United States, the (then) Soviet Union, and any other country not approved of by the Beijing leadership. It will be interesting to see when this text is dropped from new editions: it cannot be long.

Behaviour

Children

Tiny Chinese children are adorable, all are agreed. They toddle around drunkenly, squatting down and performing through the thoughtfully provided gaps in their trouser seats whenever and wherever they wish, and the adults coo and marvel at their prowess.

By the age of five a girl should cease to toddle and start to share in the housework, but a boy can be a toddler for twice as long before he has to take on responsibilities.

Both boys and girls are tolerated as full members of the family, not sent to bed early, nor told to be quiet, nor excluded from even the most adult discussions. If they overstep the disciplinary mark – and it takes a long stride to do so – they may be beaten severely by one of their parents and it is rare for another adult to attempt to intervene.

Eccentrics

A Middle Kingdom person can never be 'off-centre'. There are no eccentrics in China – people are either within a tolerable range of behaviour or they are stark mad and locked away as non-people.

The Elderly

Reverence for old age has been a strong feature of the Chinese psyche. They have scorned the West for its hard-hearted elbowing of the elderly out of the family and its shutting them up in twilight homes. But that reverence is less obvious in China than it was, and the day of the old people's home is dawning – except for the leadership, that is. The respect for leaders long past their sell-by date is so great that their views on all matters remain sacrosanct.

Pets

Chinese pets are treated badly. The children torment and torture them, the adults neglect and kick them or cruelly tie them up. Most pets are thin, mangy and cowed – very sensible of them in a way, for the Cantonese would certainly eat them if they looked appetising: they will eat anything with four legs, except a table or chair, anything which flies, except an aircraft, and any animal of which the back faces heaven (which lets man off the hook provided he remembers not to crawl).

Dogs get vicious at night when they bark and bite to make up for their day-time maltreatment. Of course no-one notices when they bark, and they can go on uninterrupted all night.

Only birds are well treated – if being confined in handsome but tiny cages is good treatment. They are valued for their singing but, as that is best induced by putting lots of them together so that they aggressively sing their territorial songs, many of them die of apoplexy or else spend much time covered over so that they cannot see other birds.

Obsessions

Virility

All Chinese men are obsessed with sexual performance. To ensure that they are up to the mark they watch what they eat very carefully, and no Chinese man is worth his salt who cannot list the foods which help and the foods which don't. Aphrodisiacs are detected in the most unlikely substances.

"Why do you eat that disgusting-smelling stuff?" "It's good for men." "Have some more of this delicious kale." "No thank you, it tends to reduce performance." "Do you like freshwater Shanghai crabs?" "Yes, delicious, but it's a good job they are only in season for a short time because they are weakening for men, you know." "What about guavas?" "No fear, they are for women only."

Traditional medicine shops do a lucrative trade in dried stag penises. They are sliced like carrots and boiled up into soup. Only men drink the soup, which is just as well as there is no way then to find out that it has no effect on anyone, man or woman. With great fastidiousness this delicacy is known as 'stag's tail', but if the innocent enquire why a stag's tail should be so good for men, they are politely told that of course it is 'the other tail'.

The gall bladder ripped from a living snake is also considered a helpful source of sexual potency, though whether any woman welcomes the advances of a man who has just drunk raw snake's gall is to be doubted.

Of course the greatest aphrodisiac is a woman, and the ultimate is a virgin. Chinese men are programmed to salivate at the mere thought of a maidenhead, and few disbelieve the tales of the Chinese leadership having constant supplies of young girls brought to them. "If you had that power, wouldn't you?" they say.

The Chinese share with the Malays a hysterical condition known to the medical world as Koro – the shrinking penis syndrome. When the going gets rough and men feel threatened they start to feel their penises shrinking back into their bodies. It is well known that if the penis shrinks totally away the man will die, so to prevent this he ties stones to it, or puts a clothes peg on it, or clamps it between chopsticks, or he holds it and runs shrieking to the nearest hospital for urgent treatment. In 1967 there was an epidemic of Koro in Singapore serious enough to get written up in the *British Medical Journal*.

Size, as everyone knows, has nothing to do with performance, and the old story that Peking chemist shops sell condoms in three sizes (small, extra small, and training) is without truth. However, Western men travelling to China are advised to take their favourite brand with them or else to drink only guava juice.

Kung-fu Movies

Kung-fu movies are an obsession with the Chinese all over the world. No plot is required for the films, they merely have to have baddies and goodies and ingenious technical effects.

The *kung-fu* master can leap tens of feet into the air and land safely twenty yards beyond his evil adversary who was about to decapitate him with a stream of deadly arrowheads shot from the sleeve by a spring-loaded-launcher strapped to his forearm. He conjures up dark clouds to escape in, runs faster than the baddy's sports car, and can do battle with a dozen or more heavily armed and invariably ugly thugs at once, leaving them in a bloody heap in whatever leafy glade they had used for their ambush.

When cinemas are closed there is an inexhaustible supply of *kung-fu* videos for hire or purchase, and for those dreary moments of the day when no screen (silver, wide or small) is available there is the *kung-fu* comic, luridly illustrated in more-than-full colour.

Health

Chinese people are obsessed with their health. They spend fortunes on quack remedies, bona fide doctors, alternative practitioners of a bewildering variety of arts, preventative potions and exercises, massages, special teas, pills, lozenges, bottles, sprays, inhalers, creams, balsams, oils, lotions, embrocations, plasters, droppers: in diverse forms, the Chinese have them all. Above all the Chinese have discovered the joys of the injection. Got a cold? Have a jab. Have another, it might be influenza. And come back next week for a booster in case you have been weakened by the other two. "I knew I was off colour and Dr Wang said I should have an injection, proving that I was indeed ill."

Forget the bedside manner, a doctor with needle technique can make all the money he and his family can possibly spend.

Leisure and Pleasure

The Chinese like eating, watching *kung-fu* movies, and gambling. Occasionally by way of a change they will have a snack, watch a *kung-fu* video, or have a bet. They never go on holiday. They sometimes indulge in sex.

Other possibilities are watching football, listening to caged birds, betting on crickets pulling each other to pieces, and learning just enough English to follow hapless foreigners around and repeat the same phrase at them thirty times. Parents and grandparents take pleasure in admiring their children and grandchildren. Children and grandchildren take pleasure in being admired.

Whatever activity it is, whether eating, watching, gambling, eating, listening, admiring, or eating, it must be done in company and to the accompaniment of noise.

Sex

In contrast to the West, where political leaders and Catholic priests fall from grace the minute it is rumoured that they may have been over-friendly with a neighbour, his wife or even their dog, in China sex is something which it is assumed the leadership need a lot of and which they are entitled to in as large measure as they require. Chairman Mao, it is said, had lots of young girls to help him nourish and replenish his vital forces, and if the infamous Empress Dowager (who in the late 19th century strove so hard to bring down the dynasty she represented) had had only a tenth of the lovers with which she has been credited in the popular mind, she would still have had to devote more time to bedroom activities than to those of government.

For the common people of the West, sex is all-perva-

31

sive and every person's birthright (not to mention some people's birth-rate). But in China the leadership does not seem to consider sex a proper matter for discussion or for bringing to the attention of hoi polloi. It must happen because of the size of China's population, but it is not to be flaunted or enjoyed by the masses.

What most excites a Chinese male is skin – blemish-free, hairless, smooth, sheen-emitting, pale-coloured skin will reduce a man to pulp, even if the girl happens to be wearing dirty dungarees, have her hair in tangles, and be wearing a hearing-aid and thick spectacles. Figure does not count at all, partly because figure means shape, shape comes with adulthood, and Chinese men above all like little girls. They like their women to talk in baby voices, to have skin as smooth as that on the proverbial baby's bottom, to pout and sulk like 5 year-olds, to be shy and cheeky by turns, anything rather than adult.

While Western men go for strapping wenches with long legs, big hips, narrow waists and high protruding bosoms (look at any chorus-line), Chinese girl dancers on stage show no leg, have flattened bosoms, dance with their blushing faces coyly hidden behind their sleeves, and demurely point to their maidenly dimples with oh-so-tiny hands, occasionally peeping roguishly with bright eyes at the handsome young men who are inflamed with passion for their winsome and (surely?) virgin charms.

The ideal and sexy man, if Chinese literature is to be believed, is a silk-clad exquisite, effeminate to a degree, swooning and soulful – and rich. It is true that there are more heroic types to be found in novels – swash-buckling, blood-thirsty, hard-drinking, hard-living men – but they never have relationships with women other than brief encounters with conniving nymphomaniacs and their female pimps, and both these types of women always come to a sticky end (usually at the hands of the

32

hero), while he himself is never deceived to the point of actual sexual contact. He is a good chap, the Chinese equivalent of a rugby-playing, lager-swilling extrovert, but he does not inspire illicit thoughts of sexy romps in the girlish fancy. Meanwhile his foppish, largesse-distributing cousins are carrying off all the prizes.

Again if literature is to be believed, the ideal woman has a nose like 'a suspended gall-bladder', an image lost on the outsider, but much coveted by the food-addicted Chinese. "Oh, my heart and liver, (i.e. my darling)," will sigh the amorous cuisine-inspired Chinese swain.

The greatest beauty of all Chinese history was called Xi Shi. She was so frail that she was blown over by anything stronger than the lightest zephyr; she was so light that she could dance on a lotus leaf and it would not sink beneath the waters; and her feet were so small that they could fit easily into the hand of an infatuated man.

Tiny feet came to mean beautiful and sexy. Thus footbinding was born. Carried to extremes the bindings could result in feet only three inches long, the so-called 'Golden Lotus Foot'. It didn't matter that the women were in constant pain, prone to gangrene and permanently crippled; to Chinese men, they were all beautiful. Today only a few old women remain as living memorials, hobbling around with sticks, or carried on the backs of their grandsons.

Gambling

No Chinese ever 'plays' at gambling games, he takes them far too seriously for that. Besides, 'playing' implies fun, and the Chinese as a people have gone way past the stage where they can gamble for enjoyment: they gamble for real, staking more than they can afford to lose, true addicts.

Chinese gamble on anything and everything: football, snooker, horses, roulette, fan-tan, dice, cards, mahjong, dominoes, dogs, stock exchanges, lotteries, coin-tossing, elections, currency, futures, derivatives, cricket-fighting, cock-fighting, tortoise-racing – the list is truly endless. One seller of oranges in 19th-century Canton is reported to have had a bet with his customers on the number of pips each orange would be found to contain when cut open, and he offered different odds according to how many were counted. Lucky customers could get to eat for free.

The betting on any one horse race in Hong Kong is usually greater than the total for any full race meeting in Britain, and it is not uncommon for people to be turned away from the track because it is too full.

Many Chinese will tell you that they do not gamble. You are entitled to disbelieve them. What they mean is that they have temporarily run out of funds to gamble with – you can bet on it.

Culture

China and the West

The easiest definition of Chinese culture used to be 'Chinese culture is different from other cultures'. The Chinese wrote vertically and from right to left, the West wrote horizontally and from left to right. A Chinese man shook hands with himself, Western man shook hands with others. Chinese paid their doctors for keeping them well, the rest of the world only paid them when they were ill. Chinese cooks cut everything up in the kitchen, elsewhere the eaters cut it up on the plate. Chinese theatre was based on convention, singing, improbable story-lines and stylised movements, Western theatre looked for realism and accurate reflections on and of everyday life. Chinese saws cut on the pull, Western saws on the push; Chinese planes cut towards the planer, Westerners plane away from themselves. Chinese men wore long gowns and the women wore trousers. Chinese culture invented gunpowder and made fireworks, Western culture used it to blow up the walled cities of Europe and abolish the feudal system. Chinese culture looked to the remote past as a golden age and one to be returned to if possible, other cultures looked to the future and the golden age they will enjoy when they have invented, discovered and changed everything.

Differences in Chinese culture are no longer so obvious. Industrialisation, urbanisation, and the pursuit of economic heaven have swung the Chinese more into line with other cultures. 'Socialism with Chinese Characteristics' has become a buzz-phrase and illustrates what has been happening to China over the 20th century – a trend to major alignment with the outside world but covered with a coating of cultural paint. At present, if you scratch a Chinese industrialist you will find a Chinese underneath. In a few years the same scratching will probably reveal an industrialist.

Culture With a Capital C

The vast majority of the Chinese, like the vast majority of many other peoples, do not know much about Culture. Where they have always been different is in the recognition of the importance of Culture even by those who did not participate in it. All Chinese valued and were proud of scholarship and literacy, despite the fact that throughout most of China's history probably no more than about 20% of the population could read and write. Chinese governments might despise, fear, terrorize, degrade and underpay the scholars, but the people have gone on respecting them and their education.

Chinese Culture is mostly about what does not happen in everyday life.

Chinese art shows imaginary landscapes of mists, cliffs, trees, animals and rivers with man only minimally in evidence. Real life China consists of a totally man-dominated agricultural or urban landscape where nature is only allowed to raise her head if she grows in straight rows and is edible.

Chinese drama is full of luridly-costumed, heavily-painted characters who act out stories which could never be believed beyond the stage, where gods and fairies come to humans' aid, where women are martial and not marital, where romantic male heroes fight off the forces of evil oppression with macho uprightness and are never bested by demons, carnally-inclined women or tax inspectors. Real life is not like that.

Film has taken three directions. The first is the syrupy sentimental love story, tear-jerking but almost invariably with a happy ending. The second is the social comedy, so hammed-up with mentally sub-normal policemen, grasping landlords, bribe-hungry bureaucrats and fast-talking car-salesmen that it cannot be dignified with the name satire. The third, and for decades now the most popular, is the *kung-fu* movie. Producers who have tried to move into other fields have faced instant box-office death, the only kind of reality which ever impinges on the world of Chinese film.

Chinese poetry is exquisite in its exploitation of the concentrated meanings of the Chinese script, dense imagery communicated direct to the mind of the reader to the quiet accompaniment of simple rhythms. One of the best known poems of the Tang dynasty (AD 618-907) can strike home even in translation:

> The bright moonlight shines on my bed
> It reminds me of the frost on the ground.
> I raise my head to gaze at it
> And lying back I dream of home.

The rhythms of speech are longer, harsher and more cumbersome, and the content of speech is mostly, of course, anything but poetic.

Chinese calligraphy is painting by words, another kind of visual poetry, the shapes and nuances of the written characters taking on a beauty which cannot be divorced from their meaning. Mere writing says things like 'Inflation up again' or 'Keep off the grass' and has nothing to do with visual poetry.

Chinese literature generally consisted of high-flown essays on philosophical matters, but the novel has managed to find a place (reluctantly conceded by the literati). Romantic heroes and heroines fall in love in novels, but in real life young men and young women were kept apart as much as possible and marriage was arranged by parents who were not concerned whether the couple liked each other or not. In novels mighty fighters overcame corrupt officials and bloodthirsty criminals, but in real life they were secret society thugs who collected their few dollars of protection money from half-starved street hawkers. 20th-century novelists have tried to break with the tradition, but few of them have contrived to write great literature.

There is virtually no children's Culture. Children have traditionally been thrown in the deep end with the adults, and nowadays are fed endless gouts of Walt Disney and derivatives.

Health

Tuberculosis used to be the big killer in China, but smoking-related diseases and some forms of diet-induced cancer have taken over at the top of the chart. Still, life expectancy has soared to levels very little different from those of Western Europe. The Chinese know a thing or two about health.

Medicine

The Chinese back up their obsession with health with a strong belief that if a medicine is nasty it must be good. The more revolting of the body parts of fierce animals such as tigers, bears and snakes are eagerly swallowed by the health fiend, as are animals and insects which other peoples prefer not to think of (sea-horses, the felt from stag antlers, frog warts, caterpillars, scorpions). If medicine doesn't seem unpleasant enough it can be made to look worse with colour: a greenish khaki colour is generally considered desirable. It was formerly believed that a bun soaked in the blood from a decapitated criminal's neck would cure tuberculosis: executions are now carried out with a shot to the back of the head, so it is fortunate that antibiotics are available instead.

The thermometer is the favourite toy of the Westerner who is determined not to be in full health. The Chinese find that too scientific; they prefer to talk of hot and cold as humours in the body which can be controlled by eating foods which are designated cold and hot under a somewhat arbitrary classification system. The health freak nibbles at this and sips at that in order to keep hot and cold in balance. The worst offenders are the Cantonese in the South. They have a mysterious condition called hot vapours (*yeet-hay*). It presents itself as palpitations, hot flushes, tingling, swollen lips, a burning in the stomach, and certainty of imminent death. Given the extraordinary nature of the Cantonese diet it is probably indigestion, but the sellers of the antidote 'cool tea' (*leung-char*) do very nicely out of it, thank you, and are not going to let on.

The Dawn Chorus

"Why did the sparrow-hawk? Because it saw the cuckoo-spit." The sparrow and the cuckoo should be the national birds of China. Certainly it is the hawk and the spit which herald the dawn throughout the land: the noise competes with the cockerels in the villages and reverberates through the drab corridors and air-wells of the city apartment blocks.

Beijing banned the sounding of motor-horns from the city centre some years ago: it gives the leadership comfort to be able to hear their people gearing up for another day undisturbed by the shriek of klaxons.

The Chinese are cursed with rotten noses, bridgeless and constricted, and by the time they wake up in the morning their upper respiratory tracts are so congested that only an energetic snorting, retching and expelling can give them enough air to face the day (not that the soot-laden dusty goo of Chinese cities can really be called air).

Nasal cancers are common and Chinese mockery of the 'high-nosed devils' is surely founded in consummate jealousy at the relative ease with which Caucasians breathe and smell. For their part these devils often wish that they were better protected against smelling and breathing the dust and pollution which pervade even the countryside.

Spitting is a national pastime, and the morning clear-out is actually only a sensible limbering-up for the more sophisticated activities to be indulged in for the rest of the day. The tubes must be made supple and unobstructed for the precision aim at the waiting receptacle or at the exact spot on the pavement where someone (preferably a foreigner) is about to step.

Sometimes, for the sake of variety, people blow their noses instead of spitting. No handkerchief or tissue is required. The process is a delicate ballet of fingerwork, the nostrils being squeezed then released either singly or both barrels at once, and the flying results head to join the other glistening remains on the pavements. Alas, the art has not been fully perfected by many, and not only is there danger to the passer-by from the random grape-shot of the inexpert, there is the problem of the perpetrator's fingers which also need wiping. It is probable that the tight-fitting *cheongsam* dress was devised so that there should be no tempting excess of material fluttering by at such moments.

In Xi-an beautiful blue and white enamel spittoons are provided at short intervals along the streets – this enables the citizenry to keep in practice as they go about their business. Occasional signs encourage them not to spit randomly – it is considered unsporting to fail to take aim.

Hospitals and Hygiene

Chinese hospitals are thought of as places where the sick go to die, and it is probable that death is more likely once a patient is admitted. Hygiene is not a strong point and patient care is generally left to whatever the family can manage when it visits. Much of the problem in hospitals can be simply put down to poverty.

Hygiene rarely raises its head, but it is there in unobtrusive forms. Tea, the Chinese drink, is always made with boiling water, which avoids many problems. In the South the heat drives everyone to wash all over at least once a day to rid themselves of stale sweat. In the North they are not quite so punctilious but it would be wrong to think of the people as dirty. Personal hygiene is important to them.

The relative hairlessness of the Chinese is helpful. They have very little body hair to trap sweat, dirt and germs. Many men do not start shaving until quite late in life and full beards are almost unknown. Women have little to worry about with leg hair, but it seems to be considered attractive by some to leave fluffy armpit hair on view maybe on the grounds that what is scarce is valuable.

Lavatories

For decency's sake most Chinese public toilets are marked 'Male' and 'Female', though sometimes the two entrances actually lead to the same room. Cubicles, where provided, usually do not have doors, but a people normally so prudish that their clothing will not reveal an inch more skin than is consistent with freedom of movement seem to have no difficulty with lack of privacy when it comes to calls of nature.

There is a great reluctance to waste the waste. It makes good fertilizer, and cities and towns still have their 'honey-bucket' collectors who cart the stuff away to recycle it on the fields. The job of these friends of the earth is more honourable than pleasant, except in Harbin in the north, where they leave it where it falls until savage winter freezes it solid, and then move in with picks, chain-saws and shovels to cart it away in relatively odour-free condition.

Eating and Drinking

Rice

Without eating you die, and since you have to do it you might as well make a virtue of it. All Chinese understand this, and the result has been a preoccupation with food which pervades the entire nation from Emperor to bond-servant, from Communist supremo to honey-bucket coolie.

First of all, of course, you must have enough to fill your stomach. Grain is the stuff for that, so into every child is dinned the absolute necessity to grow, preserve and treat reverently the staple crop, be it hard coarse millet, more palatable wheat, 'classier' rice, or even of recent centuries that hardy product of impoverished soils, the sweet potato.

Chinese leaders are besotted with grain production statistics and fulminate regularly against those greedy farmers who turn their backs on basic cereals and prefer to grow fruit or vegetables for high profit. Such concern is not new – an Imperial edict in 1727 launched a scathing attack on the failure of the people of Guangdong province to produce more than half the rice they consumed: 'How can it be right to look for short-term profit at the expense of neglecting the vital source of life?'

For Chinese and foreigner alike, rice is the typical mainstay of the Middle Kingdomer. The very word for 'to eat' in Chinese translates literally as 'to consume rice', and the Chinese word for food is 'Chinese rice'. A restaurant is a 'rice shop'; a dining-room is a 'rice hall'. "You have broken my rice-bowl", wails the man who loses his job or is cheated of his money. "He has an iron rice-bowl", say the envious of the man who has a secure job.

You might think that to describe someone as a 'rice-bucket' would be to compliment him – not so; it means that he is a good-for-nothing, an 'idle bastard' into whom rice is poured without anything worthwhile coming out in return.

Mothers scream at children who leave rice grains in their bowls: "Your wife/husband will have a small-pox scar for every grain you leave." So far it doesn't seem to matter that small-pox has long been eliminated.

Meals

Chinese breakfasts start quite early (5 or 6 o'clock). Thin rice porridge with severed bits of unidentifiable animals lurking or floating, oil-soaked strips of unsweetened doughnut, dishes of salty, chilli-hot pickles, and large soft cubes of coagulated pig's or chicken's blood form the backbone. Few foreigners indulge, and Chinese who travel abroad all take to English breakfast with the fervour of converts seeing light where before was only darkness.

Lunch is eaten at about 11.30 or midday. It is sometimes a snack – perhaps a bowl of noodles in soup with fish or meat pieces in – and sometimes a full multi-course meal complete with rice, bread or noodles (but only if your host's work unit is paying the bill). An hour or so's rest (called *xiu-xi*) is then necessary for digestion: only frenetic Hong Kong does not take it.

Dinner, at about 6.30 p.m., is several courses at least.

In South China the old custom of a late night supper around midnight is creeping back after decades when everyone was expected to go to bedhalf way through the evening. The fare tends to be on the exotic side – seasnake in rice porridge, ox testicles, or tasty but hideous-looking catfish, served whole with the head on.

Chopsticks

Deforestation, over-population, the mosquito, and a lack of tin have between them been responsible for the development of the world's best cuisine and its weirdest eating method.

Blame for the fact that firewood and other fuels are expensive can be laid at deforestation's door. The Chinese have got used to minimal cooking at high temperature, often using grass or rice straw which they have in plenty. By chance this quick-cooking method preserves much of the nutritional value of the food, so that they get healthy eating from their frugality.

Over-population means that labour is cheap in China, so restaurants can afford to have lots of cooks. This is just as well, because Chinese food demands a high level of preparation, each item being diced, sliced, minced, trimmed, pounded, ground, flattened, fluffed-up, drawn-out, rolled-up exquisitely by hand in order to get the optimum size and shape for a quick blast in the wok. Again by chance, all this care and attention to detail produces wonderful gourmet dishes.

The Chinese equivalent of Sheffield or Pittsburg is a city called Wu Xi. Wu Xi means 'No tin' and it seems logical to assume that it was called so because the excessive demands of a swollen population for cutlery quickly exhausted the mines. Just to make the myriad cooks of China enough kitchen knives and choppers has always kept the metal industry at full stretch, leaving no means of supplying the eaters or indeed of starting an industrial revolution. How else can one explain the fact that a culture which knew the magnetic compass, printing, the screw, gunpowder, paper, advanced mathematics and many other wonders failed to develop into a major scientific powerhouse? It was all the fault of the cooks.

People had to eat, and since they had hot food they could not use their hands. Well, then, let them use wood... but the trees had all been uprooted to make way for people and cereal crops... Bamboo, then? Fine. Bamboo is a kind of straight woody grass, it grows quickly and so is in strong supply, it is hollow so could be used to scoop up food... but it is not very easy to carve into shapes, and though it can be whittled to a sharp edge it is too thick to make a good knife. Well, why not use two pieces, one in each hand, and grab the food up rather like the gardener picks up autumn leaves with two flat paddles of wood? Brilliant... but there are still the mosquitoes.

Ah, yes, the mosquitoes. Well, you see the problem. Where there is a dining table there are mosquitoes lurking beneath it, and while people eat above the table the whining monsters take their vicarious share of the same nutriment under the table by guzzling up the peoples' blood through their sharp little probes. "Ai-ya!" cry the diners and aim a swipe at the offending insects. "Ai-ya! Ai-ya!" they cry again as the bamboo eating implement splatters five-spice sauce all over their best silk trousers.

And this brought about the final refinement, the invention of chopsticks. The two sticks were cut from slender young bamboo stems and were thin enough to be held and used in one hand, leaving the other hand free to slap away at the mosquitoes. And because the food had been so meticulously prepared in bite-sized pieces it was not necessary to have a cutting edge or a pronged tool or even a scoop. All that was needed was a bowl and the two sticks.

Ecologically splendid. Nutritionally sound. Fiendishly awkward for the clumsy paws of the average Westerner. The Chinese use them backhand, underarm, sideways, short-handled or long-handled, any way. There are no

45

rules to the game: you can use your chopsticks however you like, and if in dire need you can even spear the food with them rather than go hungry.

Delicacies

Beside the special delicacies, such as shark's fin soup and bird's nest soup, with which the Chinese regale themselves, pâté de foie gras, caviar, frog legs, truffles and sweetbreads seem tame. Shark's fin costs a fortune because sharks are dangerous to catch, and the tough fins are difficult to prepare and take a long while to cook. Bird's nest (actually a jelly-like nest-lining made by swallows from disgorged masticated fish) is even harder to obtain, and even more expensive to buy. Neither of these luxuries tastes of anything very much and both require skilful use of other ingredients to make them palatable. You pay for rarity. On the same lines a fish called the Rat Garoupa is greatly prized (and highly priced) by the southern Chinese because only a handful are caught each year.

Everyday Chinese food is so good that the gourmet in search of a treat is forced to look to real exotica, such as roasted silkworms, the stalks of winter-melons, stew made from five different types of snake (three of them poisonous), bears' paws, raw monkey brains, fermented and rotted beancurd, inch-long white maggots harvested from rice plants and cooked into an omelette, fried water-cockroaches, so-called 'hundred year-old eggs' (which in fact are preserved for about three months before the yolk turns green and the white goes a transparent brown, when they are ready to eat), goose testicles, rhinoceros horn, roast pigeon brains, braised dog meat, and the famous Cantonese speciality *Loong-foo-foong* (Dragon, tiger and phoenix) a dish made from snake, cat and chicken. Add to this list the meat of any animal, insect, fish or bird which faces extinction: that immediately appeals to the Chinese gourmet as something he must taste before it is too late.

Drinking

Many Chinese cannot tolerate alcohol; they become red in the face and hopelessly sleepy at the first sip. Those who can drink tend to do so only with food, so that alcoholism has never been a serious problem, except among poets.

Chinese poets drink, probably because trying to compose poetry in Chinese is a nightmare and only the seriously inebriated can find any semblance of a rhyme. One notable tried so hard to find a word to go with moon that he fell overboard and drowned in the river while embracing the moon's reflection in the water. His drunken spirit still haunts the waters, they say, optimistically mouthing 'soon, soon' but never quite escaping from the liquid which hadn't passed his lips until his death.

The real reason why so few people drink is that almost every variety of Chinese booze tastes dreadful. It is mostly made of coarse grains, and is distilled over and over to produce a clear firewater which smells and tastes like a mixture of linseed oil and methylated spirit. It burns the throat, mortifies the stomach, turns the bowels to putrefaction, and stays on your breath and therefore on your mind for days after the drinking has been done. There is only one way to deal with it – get drunk quickly and stay that way until welcome death bears you away to that sweet land where hangovers are unknown.

Manners

Politeness

Chinese men used to greet each other by holding their left hands in their own right hands, raising them in front of their chests, and shaking hands with themselves, but have dropped the habit almost entirely over the course of the 20th century. Both men and women tend to shake hands with foreigners, and many Chinese shake hands amongst themselves now too. Kissing is rare, and newsreel pictures of President Nixon's wife kissing Chinese children showed the children in a state of shock and some revulsion.

Family members seldom display emotion at meeting, and if someone meeting an airline passenger says nothing but merely turns on his/her heel and walks off followed by the passenger, the chances are that they are husband and wife, or mother and son, or brothers, or sisters, or brother and sister meeting again after an absence of years. Display is in inverse ratio to depth of feeling.

Strangers can be asked things which no British person would dare ask: "How old are you?", "How much do you earn?", "What rent do you pay?", "How come you have been married for two years and still have no children?" It is not impolite to ask, and you are expected to answer, though a little careful evasion or tailoring of fact may be in order. You can ask the same things, of course.

There are things which you should avoid saying for fear of embarrassment. If you are a man, do not say "How beautiful your daughter is". (The filthy beast is after my daughter.) And do not force the other person into making a gesture out of politeness. For instance, do not say too often, "What a nice picture that is on your wall". (Oh, no, he wants me to give him my Picasso.)

Social Niceties

The Chinese language has a word for Good Morning and another for Good Night, but there is nothing in between. Greetings at other times vary from a grunt to "How are you?", to stating the obvious ("Oh, you're going shopping", "Oh, you've got off the bus", "Oh, you're having a sleep"). Just nodding will not do – as always, noise of some sort is called for. Probably the most common response is "Have you eaten?" reflecting the overwhelming Chinese obsession with their stomachs, but you do not reply "No, I haven't" because it sounds as though you are asking to be taken out to lunch.

Polite forms of address used to be really complex. Another person's wife was referred to as his 'Great one' but one's own wife was 'My miserable thorn', and similarly 'Your honourable surname' but 'My little surname', 'Your mansion on high' but 'My humble hut', 'Your Prince' but 'My mendicant son'. Few people know the system any more, and less extreme politenesses are used (Your/my wife, Your/my surname, Your/my house, Your/my son).

For thirty or forty years almost everyone in Mainland China could be simply addressed as Comrade (*tong-zhi*), but this word has also gone out of fashion, and Mr, Mrs, Miss, Ms, Dr, Professor, and so on are back in favour. One new term which has stuck is *ai-ren* for spouse: *ai-ren* literally means lover and has the merit that it does not imply any inequality between the married partners.

Amongst friends nicknames are common. Quite often the names are physically descriptive and not always kind (Lofty, Rat-face, Pock-face, Slobber-chops, and Watermelon-peeler for someone with protruding front teeth). The British will not mention woodworm in front of a man with a wooden leg, but the Chinese will call him

Peg-leg and loudly complain to him of the amount of sawdust pollution nowadays.

"You go first." "No, you go first." The battle to give precedence to others can seriously clog doorways and impede the operation of lifts. Luckily such politeness only applies to people who know each other, so the problem is limited. Chinese consideration for others is immaculate when it involves kin, friends, those to whom they have been introduced, and those in a position of authority. No-one else exists.

The same person who has practically gone down on his knees to plead with his friend to go through the office door first will next minute be elbowing his way to the front of the taxi queue and pushing little old ladies into the gutter in the process. Two men on a bus will hold a raucous, obscenity-filled conversation at the tops of their voices without even noticing the presence of children and respectable people, and three people walking together along a narrow path will not go in single file to allow a stranger coming the other way to get by – he must squeeze to one side till the stronger group, unconscious of his presence, have dawdled on their way.

When the Chinese go to the cinema they converse, spit and eat scratchings (talk, hawk and pork) as loudly as possible in order to drown out the dialogue. It is especially noticeable during a Western language film, because the audience can read the Chinese sub-titles and don't need to hear the English.

At a live performance Chinese audiences do not usually react or clap, except in the case of a particularly famous performer or much loved piece. But if an actor makes a mistake or something goes wrong with the scenery, everyone laughs uproariously.

It is polite to fight over the bill in a restaurant. If you get to pay, it hurts your pocket but you have scored a moral victory over your companions. The most sensible tactic is to slip out to wash your hands just as it is clear that the time for paying the bill is coming up. When you emerge, you bustle back to the table calling out loudly to the waiter for the bill to be given to you and not to any-one else. Someone else will, of course, have paid while you were away, but you get the credit for trying to pay and none of the pain of payment.

Table Manners

Chinese people eat to enjoy themselves and do not wish to be hedged about with footling restrictions. You can talk with your mouth full. It can hardly matter if food taken from communal bowls happens to be accidentally spat back into them in the course of an excited diatribe.

You may slurp your soup. In fact, the noisier the better, it shows how much you are enjoying it. And, of course, slurping sucks in air to cool the soup, so that you don't need to indulge in that disgusting Western habit of blow-ing on it in the spoon. Also some of that same air may be conveniently swallowed in order to provide sufficiently hearty burping material.

You burp if the mood takes you. There is no need to apologise because no-one will hear and no-one will notice.

If you feel like having some of those noodles from the bowl on the other side of the table, you may stand up, reach over, grab a chopstick-full and carry it back drip-ping over cloth and other dishes to your own bowl, then suck it in with as loud a slurp-plop as you can contrive.

If you need a cigarette, light up. The rest of the company are just about to try the most delicate concoction of bird's nest and wren's tongue in stickleback caviar, but it won't mar their taste sensors or spoil their enjoyment.

As for 'don'ts' they are very few. Don't hide your non-chopstick hand under the table except when mosquito-hunting: people will wonder what you are up to. Don't put your fingers in your mouth under any circumstances. If you have a bone or a pip or a bit of something horrible to get rid of, spit it out on to the cloth or the floor. Every child knows that it is dirty to put fingers in mouths.

Don't use chopsticks left-handed. It's not a matter of superstition, or ergonomics (there is no such thing as a left-handed chopstick), it is common sense. A left-handed chopsticker sitting on the right of a right-handed chop-sticker is bound to get involved in chopstick-clashing; stick-clashing means dropped and wasted food, anger, insults, arguments, and fighting (soy sauce bottles at point-blank range, sometimes). None of that offends against table-manners, but it takes time and the food gets cold, so don't do it.

Sense of Humour

The Chinese like puns, wordplay, tricky variations on well-known phrases which tickle their imagination. They like gently making others feel uncomfortable with innu-endo, so that the shy and inexperienced blush and giggle. They like slapstick, they like banana-skin jokes, and they love to see the proud humbled in anecdote. They like long stories which end without punchlines, they feel somehow that inconsequence must at least be vaguely amusing.

One of their much loved comic characters is Afanti, a man of the minority Uighur people. One day Afanti goes to his landlord and asks to borrow a wok as he has guests coming and his own one is not big enough to cook all the food in. The landlord says yes, and a few days later Afanti returns bringing two woks, the original and a tiny one. "While I had it in my care your wok gave birth to this little one, so I am returning that as well", he says. The landlord gleefully accepts the simpleton's offering. Some time later Afanti again comes and asks if he can borrow the landlord's biggest wok and of course is told yes. Many days go by and eventually Afanti returns empty-handed and sad of face. "Alas, your poor wok!" he laments, "It died." "What nonsense, everyone knows that woks can't die." "If they can give birth they can surely die," says Afanti, and calmly walks away.

Custom and Tradition

The Chinese long ago decided that individuals were not the basic units of society, families were. So individuals did not have birthdays, they celebrated the increase in their ages with everyone else at the lunar New Year. The big family festival has always been the New Year, now renamed the 'Spring Festival' in Mainland China. It is a time for eating, and the first day of the year is devoted to vegetarian foods. A recent attempt to find out how many families observed this devotion produced a 100% response along the following lines: "Yes, we ate vegetarian food on New Year's Day and we also had duck, and pork, and pigeon, and ..."

Another family festival is *Ching Ming* (Clear and Bright), the grave-sweeping festival, when the ancestral graves are cleaned and offerings made to the occupants. Ancestors are believed to take an interest in the life and prosperity of their descendants, and at the same time they are dependent upon being sacrificed to in order to maintain their spiritual existence. Without the offerings of the living the dead become hungry ghosts who are likely to take vengeance on those who are depriving them. The Communist Government renamed *Ching Ming* 'Memorial Day for Revolutionary Martyrs', but that still provided enough excuse for those who believed to go on worshipping their ancestors at the graves.

The Chinese colour for death is white not black, and mourners dress in the plainest undyed clothing. An exhibition of howling and weeping is expected of close family members. Until the 20th century sons and daughters were required by law to stay in mourning for 27 months, during which time they ate only vegetarian food, wore only plain clothes, abstained from alcohol, sex, and shaving, and ideally camped out on the new grave. Few ever observed such strict mourning despite the law. Now cremation has put an end to grave-sweeping, and modern life-styles cannot allow extended mourning, but any loss to the family remains a sad and serious matter.

Colours

For the Chinese, white is for mourning and death, red for weddings and auspicious occasions, yellow for emperors and for China, green for cuckolds, blue/turquoise for what is natural and proper, and black for severe moral uprightness. Brown hardly exists at all, red passing seamlessly into yellow via orange.

Red can be seen in abundance at the celebration of National Day, 1st October. The Communists have certainly not suffered from the coincidence that their symbolic colour is the same red as that which has always been dearest to the hearts of the Chinese.

Systems

The miracle is that much of China works.

Even in the dark days of the Great Proletarian Cultural Revolution (1966-1976) when central government was virtually non-existent, somehow food continued to be produced and supplies seemed to get where they should go, businesses operated in some fashion, and the raging anarchy of the young and the politically wild went on within a shaken system which by and large still coped. Chinese people and Chinese governments fear disorder (*luan*) more than anything else, and that fear was bound sooner or later to wear down the hotheads and bring them to their senses.

State-run enterprises are infuriatingly slow and those who run them have neither concern nor time for the people whom they allegedly serve. One of the biggest jokes over much of the period of Communist rule since 1949 has been the ubiquitous slogan *Wei ren-min fu-wu* (Serve the People). How little attention is paid to it can be discovered on the first occasion you queue (or rather fight) for a railway or airline ticket. The rise of the independent private business has transformed the notion of service and made shopping far more pleasurable, but it has had little impact on the arrogant, surly, and uncaring state employees.

Plumbing has not yet been invented in China. Electricity supply is wilful and power cuts frequent. Telephones are few, except in the cities and the entrepreneurial South where the use of portable telephones has become a status symbol. Banks will do their best to prevent you from paying in or taking out money, but have somehow from time to time contrived to lend lots of money to the wrong people at the wrong interest rates. Buses are always crammed to bursting, and so are trains.

The latter run on time thanks to ingenious timetables which are based on the walking speed of China's senior leader of the moment. It is usually faster to go by bicycle, of which China has a vast number. Air travel internally is as exciting as a roller-coaster ride and ten times as dangerous.

Driving

Chinese drivers have not yet come to terms with the lowering of their status. They used to be the elite of the workforce, storming through the streets in dark glasses and deliberately terrorizing pedestrians, horses, and straining coolies struggling to pull overloaded carts. The horn was their greatest joy, though no-one seemed to hear it.

Now lots more people have certificates to say they have passed the driving test (you can buy anything in China), and there are even private cars to be seen; roads are being widened and de-rutted; white lines are being painted everywhere. The driver has become commonplace. He still sounds his horn, never observes the traffic lanes, and never gives way to another vehicle unless it is bigger than his own, but in his heart he knows that his days of glory are numbered.

Education

There are kindergartens, primary schools, junior schools, middle schools, and universities, with a range of special schools for the especially talented (or children of the leadership). Although the educators are appallingly badly paid, the system is not so bad that it does not throw up many brilliant and dedicated scholars.

Russian used to be the first foreign language but English is now overwhelmingly the one which is taught. A constant hazard for foreigners in China is that they are approached at all hours of day and night and engaged in English conversation.

Crime and Punishment

China has been trying to bring in a properly constituted legal system, and there is a growing corps of trained lawyers, but those accused of crime are seldom defended with vigour, their representatives often asking for lighter sentencing rather than refuting the charges. It does not help that the leadership has been unable to prevent itself from reserving the right to decide that someone is a criminal just because they don't like what they say or do.

Chinese police are not greatly in evidence on the streets. There are several different police bodies, some of them relatively benevolent and others decidedly sinister. If you want to know the time, buy a watch.

Punishments are heavy. Labour camp (thought-reform camp with penal servitude) and the death penalty are frequently resorted to. A majority of the population would probably agree that stiff punishments are needed, even if they believe that sometimes the wrong people suffer. The goods produced by the camp prisoners go to swell China's exports. The spare parts from those who have been shot find their way into the waiting bodies of the wealthy of Hong Kong and Southeast Asia, who are lined up in nearby hospitals on execution days.

Politics

China is a socialist state. The Chinese keep telling everyone it is. It might appear a weird mess of capitalist competitiveness, entrenched privilege of the Communist Party elite, and grinding exploited poverty, but what one is really seeing is 'Socialism with Chinese characteristics'.

There is only one political party that counts, the Chinese Communist Party. Elections are window-dressing that no-one takes seriously: if there were doubt about who would win they would not be held.

To be a member of the Party used to be considered the highest honour, but there has been a rapid falling away from this view during the late 1980s and early 1990s. Party members double up with other functionaries in almost all walks of life to try to ensure the political correctness of Chinese life, but a growing number of people are doubtful about the effectiveness of the Party and about the personal integrity of its members. Corruption is widespread and growing.

The strongarm of the Party is the army, the People's Liberation Army. It is a huge and now fairly well-armed force, and entry into it is something of an honour. During the long years of struggle against the Japanese (1937-1945) and the Nationalists (1945-1949) the PLA acquired enormous prestige as a dedicated, popular army which could be relied on not to exploit the populace it was fighting for. The fourth of June 1989, when the PLA turned its weapons on students and workers demonstrating for democracy in Tiananmen Square, destroyed that reputation outside China, but within the country itself publicity was low and a majority of the people probably had little sympathy with the demonstrators and welcomed the return to order brought about by the action.

The same fear of disorder partly explains the continued

support which the population gives to leaders who have long lost their competence to rule. Keeping them in positions of power is very reassuring, hierarchy is undisturbed, order is being maintained; it feels safe.

Business

Trade

After thousands of years when the merchant was derided as the lowest order of mankind, the Chinese have discovered that trade is good and that the trader can be a national asset.

Unfortunately, the leadership spent forty years trying to create a docile, obedient population which would take orders from the top and not think for itself. The result has been a workforce which, in return for total job security (the iron rice-bowl), dares not show initiative and works only to order, and such an attitude does not suit the new entrepreneurs. They are busy retraining people to think for themselves and to take responsibility for their own actions and for quality control. Of course, these workers can also get the sack now, which does tend to concentrate the mind.

Individuality had never been far below the surface in the old trading areas of the south and east coast and it is here that there has been a rapid readjustment to the new old ways. Now the telephone-toting, restaurant-rousting, new men of business coast around in their smart Mercedes or Japanese cars, a pretty girl or two hired from a ballroom or sauna bath establishment gracing the back seat, talking business non-stop as they eat, drink and fornicate.

It would be too much to expect that all these new get-rich-quick merchants should be honest. Their own mothers and grandmothers know better and to their cost. The funds which they invest are often not theirs, the facilities they use belong to the state or the city, but the grateful palms they grease do not wave in the direction of authority to draw attention to their crimes. On present showing, few merchants will be at the giving end of the flourishing surgical spare parts trade.

Shopping

The Chinese have always loved to haggle. Government attempts to introduce fixed prices have been successful, but outside the controlled stores old ways prevail. Pedlars can usually be persuaded to knock a little off, and the customer can have an easy conscience about beating them down because no trader would sell at a loss.

Sellers cheat. They inject meat with water to make it heavier, fiddle the yardstick with which they weigh your goods, put grit in the rice, add a bead or two to the amount which the abacus says you should be charged. But even among sellers there is honour: it is a well known fact that you are always given the right change.

Language and Gestures

Body Language

The Chinese use the 'thumbs up' sign in the same way as other nations. It is often called in Cantonese *Lum-bar Wun* (Number One). The opposite is not 'thumbs down';

it is the little finger held crooked up in the air, standing for Number Nine (bad, unlucky). The origin is supposed to be the policy which insisted that emigrant boats (Yellow slave traders) sailing out of Hong Kong in the 19th century must carry eight coffins in case of deaths during the passage. If a ninth person died he would have to be buried without a coffin, so that was bad.

When a Chinese beckons to someone such as a waiter, the hand is held palm downwards and all four fingers are waved; it would be rude to hold the palm upwards and beckon with the index finger only. Bring me the bill, please, is the universal 'signing in the air' gesture.

Spoken Language

There are many different Chinese languages, but they are all related to each other even if a speaker of one is unintelligible to a listener of another. They are all tonal languages, that is, they are sung rather than spoken. This makes the Chinese the greatest musical nation on earth, reducing the Welsh to insignificance.

Any sound can be sung in different ways to give different meanings. In Mandarin, which of all the Chinese languages has the simplest system with just four tones, the sound *gu* sung in its four ways can mean solitary, a bone, a valley, and to turn the head. Tone-deaf foreign students of Chinese have a hard time, but if there are tone-deaf Chinese they somehow manage to overcome the problem.

Because the showing of strong emotion is rare in Chinese culture, the language is not well kitted out with words to emote with. On the other hand it has lots of words for rice in all its different varieties and many stages of production.

But what Chinese really excels in is homophones (dif-

61

ferent words pronounced exactly the same as each other). English has bier/beer, pear/pair/pare, and so on, but Chinese can have dozens of words with a shared pronunciation. For instance, for the sound *gu*, in just one of its four tones, the following meanings are given in a standard dictionary: ancient, to gurgle, to explain archaic or dialectal words in current language, a valley, a gorge, cereal, 'a surname', a thigh, a section, a strand, a bull, a framework, a merchant, cobalt, a legendary venomous insect, a target, a drum, a hub, distension of the abdomen, blind. The punning possibilities are endless.

The Chinese have a genius for creating words for new concepts. English goes haring off to Latin or Greek when confronted with the need to make a new word, but Chinese just adapts an old word. *Dian* was the word for lightning, but it was used for electricity when the need arose, and then combined with other old words to order – lightning chariot (tram), lightning speech (telephone), lightning child (electron), lightning seeing (television), lightning report (telegram), lightning pond (battery), and so on. It makes new ideas seem rather less frightening.

Unlike English and other European languages Chinese does not alter the form of its words under any circumstances. Once you have learned a verb (*pao* – to run, for instance) you know it in all its uses. English contorts 'run' into runs, ran, will run, was running, would have been running, and so on, but *pao* does not change. The Chinese language makes no distinction between he and she, and it has a special set of words which classify nouns by shape or type. That is why Chinese people attempting to speak English come up with 'Pidgin English' sentences like "That piecee man she run so fast".

Pidgin has given the English language a few words such as look-see, long time no see, no can do, chop-chop, typhoon, chin-chin, but not many English words have passed into Chinese (other than into the Cantonese spoken in and around Hong Kong with its century and a half of British influence). Two important exceptions are *tea* and its variant *char*, both of which were originally Chinese words: the impact of tea on British culture in particular has been enormous.

Of Chinese concepts probably only Face has really caught the imagination of the West and found its way into speech. Everyone knows that 'to lose face' is to sink in others' opinion of oneself. Oddly, the Chinese have now started using *Fay-see* (Face) instead of the native word *Leen*, reimporting the notion of Face as if it were a foreign concept.

Swearing is widespread and almost every single swearword is an obscenity covering parts of the male and female body and things which can (and sometimes physically cannot) be done with and to them. Some ingenious people can string three or four of these words together and punctuate their conversation at frequent intervals (such as every other word).

Blasphemy is hard to commit because the Chinese attitude to gods is not reverent enough to make a contrast. But wishing the family ill is quite close to blasphemy, and "May your whole family come to grief" will give far more offence than telling you to perpetrate extraordinary acts of incest with your grandmother.

Women tend to use a set of non-obscene mild swearwords which would seem tame on the lips of a man, but some women can outswear men and are held in great awe.

Written language

The Chinese neglected to invent an alphabet, saddling themselves with a writing system which is so hard to learn that it is a wonder they did not abandon it and start again.

Instead of using a small and simple set of symbols (letters) to spell out the sounds which they made when they spoke, they decided to use much more complicated symbols (characters) to represent the ideas in their heads when they spoke the sounds of their language. But there are thousands of ideas even in primitive heads, let alone in the heads of a highly civilized people with a long long history, so they had to invent thousands of symbols. There are over 50,000 characters in existence, and there may well need to be thousands more as time goes by.

With an alphabet even a bad speller can usually contrive to communicate, but with Chinese characters there is almost no room for error. You either can remember several thousand characters and write them down correctly or you are illiterate.

Some characters are pictures, some of them are abstract constructions, some of them are just arbitrary symbols with no internal clues to their meaning. They are fun. They are a nightmare to learn. They are addictive. They slip from the memory on a bad day and refuse to pop up when called for. They seduce with beauty. They reduce foreigners to a sense of permanent inferiority before their monstrous never-to-be-mastered bulk.

Chinese educational methods are of necessity based on rote learning and repetition of facts until burned in. The mental power absorbed by becoming literate is frightening, but it certainly trains the memory: few Chinese bother with writing down phone numbers, they remember them after one hearing.